Metamorphosis

Patricia Newman

Contents

Acknowledgements

Thank you to the people who helped brings this book to completion. I am grateful to all of them.

Through Metamorphosis, I have met exceptional people who have improved my life and will remain friends forever.

Donna Armanasco (1960-2019) contacted me in 2015 and significantly impacted my life. I will never forget her kindness and knowledge. Donna said affinity brought us together. It is affinity that connects us to everything. Donna was so special. I am lucky to have known her, if only for such a short time.

I would also like to thank the new keeper of Roberts work Tin Yi Loh for her support in reviewing this book and giving her permission to print it.

A special thank you to my daughter Sheree Vickers and granddaughter Victoria Vickers, I kept changing things, and they repeatedly read everything. I would never have finished this book without them.

I want to thank my husband Royston Newman for his patience.

Thank you, John Broom, for your help and all my lovely family and grandchildren for their enthusiastic email support.

Finally, I want to thank Barbara Westgate for always being there, encouraging me with her positive feedback.

Endorsements

"This book unveils the essence of a healing art both simple and profound. Staying true to Robert St. John's teachings, Patricia reveals the anomaly between the ease in which Metamorphosis is experienced and the potentially powerful results of the practice. She adeptly takes the reader on a journey inward to help them discover the means in which they may find their authentic self."

Barbara Westgate Canada

"I think it's wonderful to have all this important work collected together. This is a quality legacy of a lifetime's work which will improve and enrich the mental and emotional well being of so many people."

Jane Pierce England

"This book has been the most helpful resource to date. Patricia clearly explains the teachings of Robert St John. Whether you are a practitioner or someone that just wants to bring a change to your life, this book will provide you with an in-depth knowledge of Metamorphosis."

Vivien Broom England

"Thoroughly enjoyed reading this very informative book."

Sheree Vickers England

"Patricia Newman's new book on Metamorphosis is a welcome addition to the few books written about this subject. What it adds to the written works is a detailed and comprehensive description of the development of 'Metamorphosis', the theory behind it and the ways to work with feet, hands, and head plus the symbols. This amount of clear detail and answers to anticipated questions has not been written before. Patricia has years of practical experience behind her plus she carried out a detailed correspondence with Donna Armanasco to whom Robert left the copyright of his work to make sure her book was accurate. There is even a long quotation from an email in which Donna explains her reasons for adding the new Creation symbol ll which should satisfy those who found it hard to accept this as part of the work. Patricia has managed to cover everything in a good read which should be of use to practitioners wanting to revise as well as newbies wanting to know how to approach Metamorphosis."

Angie Lyndon Metamorphosis Practitioner Fremantle Western Australia

Foreword

I have been practising and teaching 'Metamorphosis' since 1998. This book aims to enhance people's knowledge of Robert St. John's work and adhere to his teaching and principles, giving him the acknowledgement and the credit for his original work, 'Prenatal Therapy' and later work 'Metamorphosis'.

Donna Armanasco worked closely with Robert St. John. During his lifetime she attended lectures with him and on his behalf. Knowing she had an innate understanding of the essence of 'Metamorphosis', Robert St. John bequeathed his works to Donna Armanasco.

Donna Armanasco understandably had first-hand knowledge of 'Prenatal Therapy', 'Metamorphosis' and the hand symbols which she advanced by adding Creation 11.

Donna Armanasco approved this book knowing the teaching is factual and adheres to Robert St. John's principles.

Sadly, Donna Armanasco passed away in May 2019. The new keeper of 'Metamorphosis' is Tin Yi Loh. All works using Robert St. John's quotes or pictures should have her permission to use them.

During the compilation of this book, I emailed Donna Armanasco at various stages and she would reply with comments. From time to time, I will use excerpts from her replies as I feel they give a clear insight into Robert St. John's work.

This book relates to 'Prenatal Therapy' and Robert St. John's revised work on 'Metamorphosis'.

They are not two separate modalities; the essence of his work remains the same.

Robert St. John's early work, 'Prenatal Therapy' is in the first chapters. To understand the developments, you should know about 'Prenatal Therapy' before learning his revised work.

Patricia Newman

Robert St. John 1914-1996

Robert St. John was born in London on the 21st May 1914. He travelled extensively during his lifetime, giving lectures to his followers worldwide.

In my opinion, he was ahead of his time a great thinker his aim was to help people to help themselves, without expecting fame and wealth from his work and knowledge.

People who knew him note that he did not have an ego; he did not like to be considered special or be put on a pedestal.

During the last weeks of his life, he went to Turin in Italy to hold lectures to enhance people's knowledge of his work.

Sadly, Robert St. John died shortly after arriving in Turin on the 1st November 1996.

Donna Armanasco went to Turin to collect his works so that they would not be lost.

What is 'Prenatal Therapy'?

'Prenatal Therapy' is a gentle approach to self-healing and personal development which can help release inherited blocks and behaviour problems by working on the reflex points of the feet, hands and head which relate to corresponding points on the spine.

Conception is one of the most traumatic things we experience. From the moment of conception, everything in that first cell determines who we are and who we will become.

St. John's work teaches that we inherit traits and patterns of behaviour at conception which cause blockages that cause problems throughout our lives.

A person carries traits and stress patterns inherited at conception into their future life which inhibits them from living their lives to their full potential, free of unwanted habits and behaviour problems.

Due to their inherited disposition, many people have problems concerning their mother or father or with relationships in general.

A person who has an inherited tendency towards nervousness, whose environment is not peaceful in the womb, will feel threatened, enhancing their nervous disposition.

A person with a nervous disposition does not have the confidence to stand up for themselves; they can be overlooked for promotion; worry about everything; let their partners and others intimidate them. They will be afraid to do anything adventurous or do anything that would enhance their life.

If a person's inherited tendency were to feel unwanted, they would carry those feelings throughout their life and lack self-worth. The baby picks up its mother's feelings and other outside influences. If the baby feels unwanted, this will reinforce the inherited patterns.

A person who feels unwanted will think their siblings are the favourites. They may be the one who does more for their parents as they strive to feel needed.

Recent studies confirm that obesity and alcoholism often run in families, this verifies that inherited patterns are with us from conception.

We have an inborn intelligence called our innate intelligence; it is within us from conception until we die. It creates a state of stability to deal with both internal and external changes. It keeps us alive, in a state of optimum health internally, allowing the body to heal.

The person's innate intelligence, their life force energy flowing through them, frees them from past influences and patterns of behaviour, transmuting them from who they were to who they can be in the future, allowing them to reach their true potential.

Imagine this innate intelligence flowing throughout our body blocked by traits that we inherited at conception. If we did not remove those characteristics, life force energy could not flow freely, and we cannot move on. We remain trapped in old patterns of behaviour.

Imagine having those blocks removed. It would be as effective as removing the wall from a dam, and the life force would flow as nature intended.

It is not a technique or a treatment as this implies intent to do something. We allow it to happen, we do not direct or aim to heal, it does not cure, it simply creates balance and harmony in a person, making them healthier and happier.

When working on the reflex points, you draw the person's innate intelligence to the blocks allowing them to heal themselves. If you intend to heal, you focus on the symptoms, and then you are directing healing.

A person moves forward in a way that is beneficial to them because it is self-directed. Unlike other healing methods, we are a catalyst, we do not interfere with what is to be or take credit for the changes that occur.

The Mother/Father Principle

St. John started as a Naturopath. Along with many other holistic practices, naturopathic physicians believe the body uses innate intelligence to heal itself.

In the mid-1950s, he became interested in 'Reflex Therapy' (later renamed 'Reflexology').

He saw his 'Reflexology' clients, whose outward symptoms would disappear, requesting further sessions as their symptoms returned or presented different symptoms.

His clients' behaviour led him to believe that there was an underlying cause for the symptoms that needed investigating. St. John then began to focus his studies on the cause of the symptoms.

St. John knew that many of the ailments found in the feet could be related to corresponding reflex points situated along the bony ridge of the feet, hands and head. He found that working on the reflex points had the same effect as treating the whole foot.

He then became aware that 'Reflexology' worked on a physical map of the body. There was also a psychological map where the reflex points on the feet, hands and head corresponded to points on the spine.

Through his 'Reflexology' studies, he realised that the spine registered the time spent in the womb, known as the gestation period.

Further studies led him to discover the Mother/Father principle which enriched his theory of the psychological map of the gestation period.

The Mother Principle:

St. John noticed clients would speak about their mother while working on the heel area, often becoming emotional. They related memories and stories connected to their mother and even their birth.

St. John concluded that if there are inherited blockages in the heel area relating to birth, the person may lack maternal and caring instincts. The person's relationship with their mother could be complicated; they may also be ungrounded and out of touch with reality.

The Father Principle:

The area around the first joint of the big toe corresponds to the spine, the central nervous system. The nerves come from the brain into the spinal cord; there is no separation between body and mind.

Whilst working on this area, he observed that clients often spoke about their father. They sometimes recalled memories that they had previously forgotten.

He realised that if there are inherited blockages in this area, they could have problems with their father figure. They may have issues with authority or even with their parenting skills. This person may lack belief in himself and question his right to exist at all.

The Mother/Father Principle further confirmed St. John's theory that blockages inherited at conception were connected to a map of the nine months spent in the womb and could cause our unwanted inherited behaviour patterns in later life.

St. John realised the nine months we spend in the womb represent a time structure. By working on our reflex points, we can adjust that time structure.

Adjusting the time structure allows the person's life force to alter past traits, releasing them, allowing them the inner freedom and the ability to change and heal themselves.

St. John then advanced his theory by creating charts that superimposed a psychological map upon the 'Reflexology' map already in existence.

St. John's charts of the gestation period vary slightly from the known stages.

Pre-conception: The pineal gland is at the top of the nail. The pineal gland receives the thought patterns in time and space. The pituitary gland is at the base of the nail. It interprets these thought patterns, so they are then understandable to the mind.

Conception: The corresponding reflex point of the foot is the first joint of the big toe. The corresponding point of the spine is the 1st cervical vertebra.

Post conception: The corresponding reflex point is on the bony ridge in the area of the ball of the foot. The corresponding point on the spine is the 7th cervical vertebrae.

Quickening: The corresponding reflex point is along the bony ridge in the centre of the foot. The corresponding point on the spine is the 9th thoracic vertebrae.

Pre-birth: The corresponding reflex point is along the bony ridge to the area in front of the ankle bone. The corresponding point on the spine is the 2nd lumbar vertebrae.

Birth: The corresponding reflex point is behind the ankle, where the Achilles tendon meets the bone. The corresponding point on the spine is at the base of the spine, the coccyx.

What may you experience during a session of 'Prenatal Therapy'?

What sensations might you feel?

Everyone may experience the blocks in the reflexes differently. Some people feel heaviness in their fingers, their fingers may feel hot or cold, or their fingers may tingle. Some people feel tired, their arms may feel heavy, others may experience pain in their body. Some people do not notice anything at all.

When I start to work on an area, my fingers feel as if they are not flowing freely. It feels like the area is sticky, but my fingers flow more freely as I continue to work. You may or may not notice this, but if you do and the feeling remains when you have finished working on the area, it means the person needs more sessions. Sometimes the recipient is aware of sensations; they may tell you what they are experiencing.

St. John felt you did not pick up negativity with 'Metamorphosis' as he associated the feelings with working symptomatically. They are not associated with 'Metamorphosis' as we are working much more abstractly.

Inherited Memories versus Suppressed Memories

At this stage, I would like to clarify the differences between the two memories.

A Suppressed Memory

A suppressed memory is something that has happened to us in our lifetime. Our subconscious mind hides the event from us if it thinks it is too painful for us to cope with the trauma.

Suppressed memories leave a person with anxiety which they must find a cause for, something tangible to replace the anxiety. They may develop a phobia or an unwanted habit.

The problem is the cause; the way you deal with it is the effect. If the person can release this memory, the cause will go, and so will the effect.

An example of a suppressed memory is a client who consulted a therapist because he was afraid of needles. He was offered a post abroad which required him to be vaccinated. The therapist noticed the client had several tattoos. She asked him, "How did you have tattoos if you are afraid of needles?" He replied, "It is only doctors that I am afraid of."

During his therapy, he regressed to being a 3 year old child. A doctor was about to take a blood sample, he recalled him putting a band on his arm and he started to get upset, crying and screaming. His mother had to hold him down while the doctor took the blood sample. So, now we know it was not the needle it was the band. He told his mother the outcome of the therapy and she confirmed it did happen. So, now he had established the cause, his phobia was cured.

Inherited Memories

An inherited memory is a memory we came into life with. Therefore, we have no recollection of it. Also, this memory has a cause and effect; releasing it removes the cause and the effect.

Prenatal Therapy
Reflexes and corresponding points on the spine

The Pineal and Pituitary glands represent Pre-conception.

The Pineal gland receives the thought patterns.

The corresponding point is the top of the big toenail.

The Pituitary gland interprets the thought patterns.

The corresponding point is the base of the big toenail.

1st Cervical-Conception

The corresponding reflex is the first joint of the big toe.

7th Cervical-Post-conception

The corresponding reflex is along the bony ridge to the ball of the foot.

9th Thoracic-Quickening

The corresponding reflex is along the bony ridge to the arch of the foot.

Sacrum-Pre-birth

The corresponding reflex is along the bony ridge to the area in front of the ankle bone.

Coccyx-Birth

The corresponding reflex is behind the heel, where the Achilles tendon meets the bone.

1st Cervical-Conception

7th Cervical-Post-conception

9th Thoracic-Quickening

Sacrum-Pre-birth

Coccyx-Birth

Created for The International Metamorphosis Association

How to give a session of 'Prenatal Therapy'

'Prenatal Therapy' on the feet

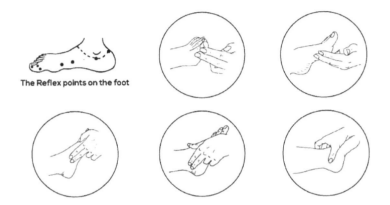

The Reflex points on the foot

Does it make any difference if you start with the right or left foot?

The right foot and hand represent the present, what we are doing with our lives. Dealing with the present clears the way to work on the past.

The left foot and hand represent the past, the inherited patterns. Working on the left foot enables our innate intelligence to make changes, to clear the blockages freeing us from unwanted behaviour patterns.

Sometimes, a person may ask you to work on the left foot or hand first, and it is fine to do as they ask.

With 'Prenatal Therapy', you are working with a circular tapping or vibratory movement covering all of the reflex points along the bony ridge of the foot.

To commence the session, start with the right foot if possible (the present). Place the foot onto your lap, observe the foot to familiarise yourself with the condition. Is the foot soft or puffy? Is the arch high or low? Does the person have hammertoes, bunions, corns or fungus on the nails? These observations may enable you to become aware of any characteristics in the foot relating to the person's inherited blockage. Characteristics found in the feet will be revisited in later chapters.

Using a circular tapping or vibratory movement, work from the top of the nail to the heel where the Achilles tendon meets the bone. return to the top of the nail and repeat the procedure.

Occasionally work from the inner anklebone, over the top of the foot to the outer ankle bone, When you are ready, end the session at the heel.

Change to the other foot to conclude the session. With 'Prenatal Therapy' the feet can only be worked on once a week to enable the person to adjust to the changes.

'Prenatal Therapy' on the hands

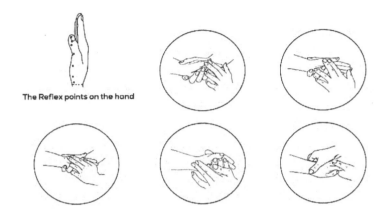

The Reflex points on the hand

Working on the reflex points of the hands will give the person the ability to handle the changes that happen.

Using a circular tapping or vibratory movement, work from the top of the nail to the wrist. Return to the top of the nail and repeat the procedure.

Occasionally work from the inner wrist bone, over the top of the hand to the outer wrist bone. When you are ready, end the session at the wrist.

Change to the other hand to conclude the session.

'Prenatal Therapy' on the head

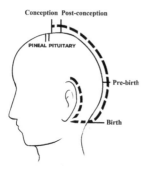

Working on the head releases our ability to think. If you fear change or have difficulty grasping the changes happening within you, working on the head enables you to use reasoning to make sense of and deal with the new patterns emerging to take control of your life.

Stand behind the person to work on the head. Using one hand to support the head, work on the head with the other hand.

You do not have to worry about staying on a reflex point on the head. Work from approximately 2cm behind the hair line to the base of the skull.

At the base of the skull, the right hand works along the bony ridge at the base, then up behind the right ear, then over the top of the right ear. The left hand works along the bony ridge at the base, then up behind the left ear, then over the top of the left ear.

When you reach the top of the ears, return to the hairline and repeat the procedure.

It is acceptable to ask the person if your hands are on the bony ridge as you work along the skull base and behind and over the ears.

Can you work on the spine with 'Prenatal Therapy'?

St. John did not work on the spine with 'Prenatal Therapy'.

Do you work on all the areas during a session?

St. John initially taught that you should look for tensions in the ankle (birth) area with a new client. He advised working on the ankle for a few sessions until the stress had gone before working on the hands or head.

Working on one area concerns me as I perceive all the areas have a function. Working on the ankle area would clear the tension and be beneficial. But, to help a person to transform all of the areas need some attention.

The function of each area involved in the transformation

The feet are the going centre. Sessions on the feet focus on the direction people take in their lives, releasing present and past traumas and inherited blockages.

The hands are the doing centre. Sessions on the reflex points of the hands will enable the recipient to handle the changes, but they need to know what the changes are to move forward.

The head is the thinking centre. Sessions on the head allow the person's inner being to make sense of the changes.

Later, St. John seemed to be confirming that all of the areas needed some attention when he advised that treatment of the feet alone can cause tension and frustrations because the thinking (head) and doing (hands) capacities are dormant and need awakening. If there is no treatment on the feet before working on either the hands or the head, there will be relatively little response because the feet will remain dormant.

Even if I work for an extended period on one area, I always spend some time on each area, but it is up to each individual how they interpret this.

What is the difference between 'Prenatal Therapy' and 'Metamorphosis'?

They share the same principles, but 'Metamorphosis' is less restricting to give and receive.

'Metamorphosis' is simple to give and receive and benefits everyone, from the new born to the elderly. However, you need to give and receive it until you feel you understand its essence.

Why did St. John revise his work?

While working with his 'Prenatal Therapy' clients, St. John observed their behaviour changed after the session.

Some clients were taking a new direction in life, others reviewing relationships and careers. They were no longer showing signs of old inhibitions and fears.

Sometimes, the client did not even realise this was happening, but people around them would comment on the changes in them.

Due to the changes it made to a person's inner being, St. John concluded 'Prenatal Therapy' was not therapy. The person was healing themselves. So, he renamed 'Prenatal Therapy' to 'Metamorphosis'.

Instead of referring to it as a therapy session or treatment, he preferred us to refer to it as sessions of 'Metamorphosis'.

Many people do not know St. John revised his work. Donna Armanasco explains why he made the changes better than I can.

Donna Armanasco (2015) explained,

> We are so used to something being produced and that thing staying the same, basically, for all time. 'Metamorphosis' is different. Before Robert died, he told me that 'Metamorphosis' would evolve even further after his death.

> They can teach the old method, but then they are missing out on a more fundamental change. Some people's attitudes of mind mean that they cannot comprehend the more abstract aspects of 'Metamorphosis' and are then compelled to stay at the level of the gestation period the more efferently orientated tend to stay with the prenatal pattern - and that's ok. I think that if someone is serious about 'Metamorphosis', then they will want to read his work, then they will decide how 'deeply' they wish to become involved.

> People believe Robert produced nothing other or after the prenatal pattern, so most people involved in 'Prenatal Therapy' don't go looking for Robert's work; it mostly just doesn't occur to them to look. People find Robert's work from 'Metamorphosis' practitioners, the internet, word of mouth and just other people who practice 'Metamorphosis' for themselves.

As a teacher of 'Metamorphosis' I immediately introduce the newer aspect of 'Metamorphosis' to my students-the old method I refer to more as an example of the chronology of his thinking, how he came to the new approach.

At one point, Robert thought seriously about scrapping his first book altogether as he said it was largely redundant. I convinced him that the importance of keeping it available to people was that it was a chronology of his thinking and that people may be interested in that. He relented and agreed. The book is still in print. His old 'Prenatal Therapy' is a bit like being in the dark in regard to 'Metamorphosis'. It does do something obviously, but it is limited.

Shortly before he died St. John wrote a letter that Donna Armanasco found amongst his personal effects. I have permission to print the letter. However, the following is just the excerpt that relates to 'Metamorphosis' that is already in the public domain.

Sometime during the middle of the, 1950's I observed several "reflexes" in the spinal reflex, as defined by Reflexology which were different from those of Reflexology.

The Reflexology reflexes are in relation to the physical parts of the body, physiological: The reflexes I was observing were not physiological, they did not have the "feel" of the physiological reflexes, they felt more abstract; in fact, I finally defined them as Attitudes of Mind.

There were seven of them: the pineal, the pituitary, the first cervical vertebrae, the seventh cervical vertebrae, the ninth thoracic vertebrae, the sacrum, and the tip of the coccyx. These seven reflexes were in the same area as those of 'Reflexology' and had the same relationship with the organs of the body, but they were different in their significance, they related to a way of thinking and feeling.

This was the beginning of 'Metamorphosis', but at that time, I called it 'Prenatal Therapy' because these reflexes referred to a period of time during the gestation period of the subject.

It did not take me long to realise that this was not a therapy, as is 'Reflexology', but a way of changing or transmuting these attitudes of mind.

I wrote a book in 1976 called 'Metamorphosis A Textbook on Prenatal Therapy'.

This book describes the fundamental and physical aspects of the reflexes and an application to them. Later on, I developed a more abstract explanation to the nature of the phenomena which these reflexes displayed (Robert St. John, 1996).

Most of the information in 'Prenatal Therapy' remains the same. St. John made the changes because he did not feel it was necessary to work within the timeline of the gestation period.

Instead of naming the reflex points:

- Pre-conception (the pineal and the pituitary glands)
- Conception
- Post-conception
- Quickening
- Pre-birth
- Birth

He renamed them:

- Pre-conception (the pineal and the pituitary glands)
- Awareness
- Concept
- Idea
- Thought
- Form
- Creation
- Action

As St. John wrote in his letter, the reflexes for attitudes of mind had the same relationship with the body's organs as 'Reflexology', but they differed in their meaning. They related to patterns of the mind which determine our way of thinking and feeling.

The baby's attitude of mind governs the mother's physical, mental and behavioural states during the pregnancy and birth. It is the baby's attitude of mind towards life that determines the nature of its birth.

Replacing the gestation period with attitudes of mind to loosen the time structure was a much more abstract approach to St. John's work.

St. John did not put much emphasis on the feet with his revised teachings. With the prenatal pattern, working on the feet more than once a week could bring on a kind of nervous depletion because the prenatal way deals with a time structure that takes time for us to process.

Working with attitudes of mind removes the restrictions of a time structure, allowing people to work on themselves and others as often as they wished.

The difference between Prenatel Therapy and Metamorphosis are St. John renamed the Reflexes, holding the reflex points, and working on the feet as often as you wish to.

'Prenatal Therapy' taught us to work over the reflex points with a circular, tapping, or vibratory movement.

In 'Metamorphosis', St. John did not use circular, tapping, or vibratory movements as he believed that this was more aligned with and leftover from his work with 'Reflexology'.

St. John taught placing our fingers on the reflexes was more direct and effective.

To strictly adhere to St. John's teaching of 'Metamorphosis', we should hold the reflex points. Donna Armanasco believed that as St. John taught, there are no rules; we should have an informed choice to decide which method to choose.

Whether to hold or use the circular action is up to the individual. The subconscious does not have any preference where on the physical plane you work. The intention is not to clear these blockages; it is the recipient's life force that does that work.

If the recipient is pregnant, it is advisable not to hold the reflexes on the ankles, use the circular movement instead (Refer to 'Metamorphosis' and Pregnancy).

Afference and Efference

St. John studied the 'Bates System of Eyesight Training'. This teaching was the foundation for his work with attitudes of mind.

This system taught:

- Hypermetropia is the inability to focus on the near point.
- Myopia is the inability to focus on the far point.

He concluded that the attitude of mind that created Hypermetropia was a withdrawing or retreating attitude, pulling away from seeing, creating a pulling back of the eyeball which he later named afference.

Myopia was an outgoing attitude: a forcing forward of the eyeball forcing a person to go forward; he later referred to this as efference. He felt the mind created both conditions after arriving at this theory; he did not know how to put it into practice. When he was developing the Prenatal Pattern, the solution came to him. He realised the change had to come from within the subject. It was their innate intelligence that could make the change and not the will of another.

St. John observed that there are two types of personalities both react to stress differently.

One type of person hides from life, procrastinating, leaving tasks unfinished and losing motivation. The other type is driven to succeed, unable to relax, always striving to do more, causing them inner stress. St. John's revised work used the terms afference (retreating) and efference (bring forward) to describe the personalities. He taught that the philosophy of 'Metamorphosis' could be summed up with:

- Afference consciousness, the principle of life and our inner guiding principle. Meaning it is an inward action. Stress in the Karmic pattern (the thought patterns in time and space aspect, it is not the same meaning as Karma which means actions) inherited at conception can account for a person's afferent orientation.

- Efference matter the substance of life, meaning to bring forward conveying outwards or to discharge. Stress in the genetic pattern at the time of conception passed on via our paternal genes can account for a person's efferent orientation.

Although, the two Latin words do not mean compulsive withdrawal and outgoing compulsion, St. John thought they were the appropriate words to describe 'Metamorphosis'.

However, he said comparing afference to introversion or yin and efference to extroversion or yang altered the meaning of the words when relating to 'Metamorphosis'.

We are all both afferent and efferent. However, we tend to have an orientation towards one or the other in our approach to life.

It is preferred not to label anyone as being one or the other. It then can be perceived as good and bad, when primarily, this is not the case. The individual is following their patterns, the factors present at their conception. Observe them as a whole with one orientation more apparent.

Afferently Orientated

The afferently orientated person has vision and awareness. They can accept many points of view and are capable of originality, having great ideas but take little action to see them through. They think before acting, if they act at all. They want things to be different. They are aware that they should be taking responsibility for what is happening in their lives to pursue their plans, but because of their inability to act, things they should be dealing with go unattended.

The very afferently orientated tend to be very logical and not emotionally demonstrative. Others may perceive them as distant. They are oversensitive, meaning they feel the stress of life; they pick up on the psychic aspect of life and the stresses of others.

They can suffer from depression, reacting with an angry outburst when they feel misunderstood which to everyone else seems irrational, but it is not to them. Putting up with the insensitivity of others causes one last (possibly small) thing to break the camel's back.

Efferently Orientated

The efferently orientated have little or no vision and awareness. The efferently orientated can be materialist, emotionally and physically active and reactive. If this person senses stress in another person who is mainly afferent, they will feel compelled to dominate them.

The afferently orientated by taking no action, provokes the efferently orientated to act which may account for bullying, domestic violence, arguments, and general unrest.

If they become involved in a business or personal relationship, they will insist on doing things their way, taking the credit for any business success, and blaming failure on others.

Stress in the efferent pattern compels them to act without thinking things through. Their actions are compulsive which may prevent them from thinking about anything, or anyone, just reacting to situations with no thought of the consequences for themselves or others. They find it hard to grasp and fully understand afference and efference. They only have one point of view, and it is a point of view that is unbending as they strive to prove their point. They firmly believe there is nothing wrong with their actions and think that they do not need to change as it is other people who are to blame.

People have to switch between afference and efference. Their career might require them to give lectures or presentations. Many celebrities admit to having stage fright to the point of being physically sick. Once they are performing, they can cope as they have switched to efference. However, the long-term effect can be damaging to them. Their mental health may suffer. They may rely on harmful substances or medication as a coping mechanism.

When you are in the company of someone who has a different orientation, you may find you switch over to their wavelength, allowing you to adjust your thinking and behaviour.

Children who are afferent may be encouraged to be more efferent. They may not want to but adapt to a situation which can take its toll on them as it requires a lot of energy. They may be tired or feel unwell. Being unwell gives them a chance to rest and relax.

The efferently originated child fits in well, they are sociable and enjoy activities. They enjoy being the centre of attention.

Sometimes, an afferently originated person will feel they need an efferent partner to take responsibility, to make decisions. They will allow them to take action. The efferent is happy with this situation.

However, long term the efferent may become bored by the afferents preference not to take action. They may feel they are left to take all the responsibility; they will become frustrated by the lack of interaction. The afferent will find the continuous activity of their partner tiring. Being told to be more active can be perceived as nagging or criticism.

Efference and afference can cause conflict in relationships. For example, the efferent partner's sister is visiting the next week, the efferent will plan for the visit and they will be stressed until everything is ready. Their partner being afferent cannot see the urgency to take action so soon. It would be acceptable to start preparing the evening before. Another cause of conflict is the efferent partner will be ready for a meeting or appointment and waiting to leave. The afferent partner will not take action until nearer the time.

No one is wrong, and both feel the other partner is being unreasonable. 'Metamorphosis' could close the gap between them.

It is good for people who have empathy to work on each other to make relationships more harmonious. They may prefer to work on themselves which has the same outcome.

How can 'Metamorphosis' help create harmony and balance within a family unit?

Each family member will be both afferent and efferent, but one factor will be more prominent.

No one is to blame for the unconscious tensions in some family units; each member follows the pattern they inherited at conception. Afferent blame themselves, and the efferent blame others.

If several family members are efferent, there can be a chaotic environment full of tension. A mainly efferent family can be considered dysfunctional.

Families feel guilt when they admit that when an efferent family member is not at home, the whole atmosphere is more harmonious. They can relax and relate to each other without the constant attention-seeking family member upsetting and causing problems for the entire household.

Parents can relate more with one child than another, not because they favour them but because they identify with the child's inherited patterns. Families should be encouraged to give each other sessions. If they work on each other or themselves, they will benefit from a more harmonious family environment.

An afferently orientated person retreats and by doing so incites the efferently orientated to attack. The stress in the afferently orientated person creates this reaction in efference. This response may be verbal, emotional, or physical.

The afferent member could be displaying addictive or compulsive behavioural patterns. They may also be overwhelmed by the efferent member and feel undermined by their overbearing attitude, feeling they always have to comply with their wishes to keep the peace.

In contrast, the efferent member can cause tension by complaining, demanding and controlling every situation. The efferent member is powerful. They expect and demand attention; the afferent member can feel as if they are not as important, that their needs and role within the family unit are secondary.

Do twins inherit the same blockage at conception?

A study of twins has shown that one twin is always more afferent than the other; the degree varies from case to case.

At conception, they both inherited their blockage and patterns of behaviour, influencing their future behaviour.

If they are both afferently orientated they will delay taking action to be born. One twin is then driven into efference by its twin relying on it to take action and lead the way.

If they are both efferent the firstborn will take the lead and force its twin into afference by making it wait.

Throughout the baby's last month in the womb the baby is mentally preparing itself to take action to enter the world.

Caesarean induced births are often necessary for the mother and baby's safety.

The baby induced before the due date or delivered early via a caesarean has not yet completed the mental preparation for the birth.

As a guideline, unless it is an induced birth:

- Afference due to the inability to make a decision tends to arrive early or late.
- Efference will take action and arrive early or on time.

Characteristics found in the feet

The following chapter deals with characteristics in the foot which indicate inherited patterns.

St. John observed that the overall shape of the foot will tell you a great deal about the person.

Remember, you are not looking to treat symptoms; you are looking at the attitudes of mind that caused the symptoms. You cannot help noticing the symptoms that are present. It is how you view the symptom that is important.

Symptoms are an indication of the way a person functions in life due to their inherited disposition. If you look at a person symptomatically and treat symptoms instead of looking for the inherited pattern causing them; you will not be helping the person to go forward.

If a person is retreating into themselves, it is a symptom of an afferent pattern. You are not treating the fact they are retreating but the unconscious pattern of mind causing them to retreat. This person could benefit from the information about the afferent pattern, causing them to retreat and feel the way they do about themselves.

When we look at the characteristics of the foot, it is the attitude of mind which is the important thing.

Afference Patterns

The afference originated may be prone to mental health issues.

The veins are an afferent pattern. They carry blood back to the heart.

- Varicose and collapsed veins are an afferent pattern.
- Hammertoes are a sign of tension in thinking.
- High arches show a strong imagination and artistic pattern.
- A bunion located on the first joint of the big toe (conception) indicates a disturbance associated with the first weeks of gestation.
- A corn is a condition of the mind.
- The ingrown toenail relates to the pineal as this is where it occurs, indicating stress in the inherited thought patterns.

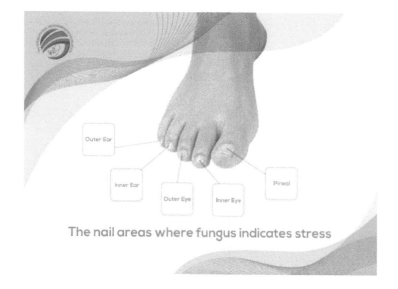

The nail areas where fungus indicates stress

- Fungus on the pineal indicates stress in the inherited thought pattern.
- Fungus on the inner and outer eye toenail indicates our ability to see within ourselves is impaired.
- Fungus on the inner and outer ear toenail indicate our ability to hear within ourselves is impaired.
- The outer eye and outer ear are outgoing which makes them more efferent.

All before the 19th week of gestation relates to the afferent pattern. All after the 19th week is related to the efferent pattern.

Efferent Patterns

Arteries take the blood away from the heart; an outgoing attitude.

- Hardening of the arteries is an efferent pattern.
- A low arch indicates an efferent pattern.
- A callus is a reaction to outgoing friction by outgoing action.
- A soft puffy foot indicates a strong emotional pattern.
- Swelling of the ankle indicates an arthritic pattern if it is a small puffy swelling directly below ankle bone.

A heart condition affects the whole ankle. To establish if it is a genetic or an inherited (Karmic) pattern you may want to ask the person if they have a heart condition.

Even though a person's behavioural patterns will change, it can be reassuring to know about behaviour patterns. It gives them an insight into their behaviour and allows them to view themselves differently.

Experience is knowledge; understanding comes from working with 'Metamorphosis'.

With other therapies, you work in a controlled way.

With 'Metamorphosis' each person presents a new experience. You are continuing to gain more insight into understanding how their inherited patterns direct them.

St. John's books have further information on the characteristics of the feet. The link to purchase them is in the recommended reading section.

St. John created new charts for 'Metamorphosis' showing the attitudes of mind reflex points and their corresponding points on the spine. To clarify the information on the 'Metamorphosis' chart, St. John does not strictly adhere to the known gestation period.

One of the stages, the quickening, is thought to occur between the 13th and the 20th week, although it may happen later. The quickening is the first time the mother is aware of the baby moving.

St. John placed the quickening at the 19th week. The corresponding point on the spine is the 9th thoracic vertebra. The reflex point is in the region of the arch of the foot.

Quickening is referred to as 'Thought' on the 'Metamorphosis' chart.

St. John referred to 'Thought' as outward development, the baby at this stage has completed its physical development; he named this the afferent stage. It now begins its outward development as it becomes aware of outside stimuli; he referred to this as the efferent stage.

We switch from afference to efference during the gestation period; at birth, we change back to the one we inherited at conception.

Attitude of Mind
Reflexes and corresponding points on the spine

The Pineal and Pituitary glands represent Pre-conception.

The Pineal gland receives the thought patterns.

The corresponding point is the top of the big toenail.

The Pituitary gland interprets the thought pattern.

The corresponding point is the base of the big toenail.

1st Cervical-Awareness
The reflex point is the first joint of the big toe.

7th Cervical-Concept
The reflex point is along the bony ridge to the ball of the foot.

5th Thoracic-Idea
The reflex point is along the bony ridge in front of the arch of the foot.

9th Thoracic-Thought
The reflex pointis along the bony ridge to the arch of the foot.

2nd Lumbar-Form
The reflex point is along the bony ridge to the area before the ankle bone.

Top of the Sacrum-Creation
The reflex point is in front of the ankle bone.

Coccyx-Action
The reflex point is behind the ankle bone.where the Achilles tendon meets the bone.

Created for The International Metamorphosis Association

How to give a session of 'Metamorphosis'

'Metamorphosis' on the feet

The Reflex Points on the feet

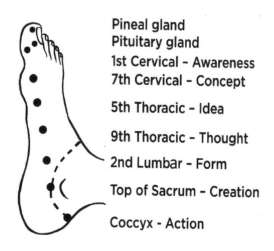

Pineal gland
Pituitary gland
1st Cervical – Awareness
7th Cervical – Concept

5th Thoracic – Idea

9th Thoracic – Thought

2nd Lumbar – Form

Top of Sacrum – Creation

Coccyx – Action

If possible start with the right foot on your lap. Familiarise yourself with the condition of the foot.

To commence the session start working from the top of the nail and touch the top of the nail and nail base.

Hold the reflex points along the ridge of the foot to behind the ankle where the Achilles tendon meets the bone. Return to the top of the nail and repeat the procedure. Occasionally work from the inner ankle bone, over the top of the foot to the outer ankle bone. When you are ready end the session at the heel.

Change to the other foot to conclude the session.

You may spend longer on one foot or hand; you may feel you need to spend more time on a specific reflex point.

'Metamorphosis' on the hands
The Reflex Points on the hands

Pineal gland
Pituitary gland
1st Cervical - Awareness

7th Cervical - Concept

5th Thoracic - Idea

9th Thoracic - Thought

2nd Lumbar - Form

Top of the Sacrum - Creation

Coccyx - Action

To commence the session start working from the top of the nail and touch the top of the nail and nail base.

Hold the reflex points along the ridge of the hand to the wrist. Return to the top of the nail and repeat the procedure. Occasionally work from the inner wrist bone, over the top of the hand to the outer wrist bone. When you are ready end the session at the wrist.

Change to the other hand to conclude the session.

'Metamorphosis' on the head

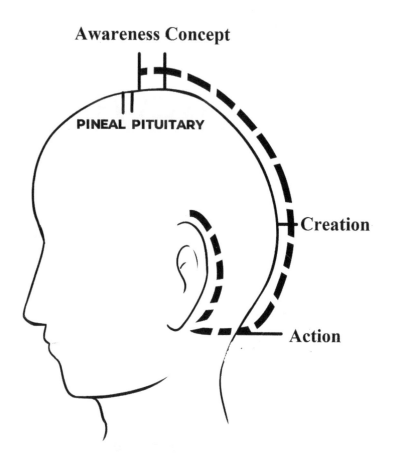

Awareness Concept

PINEAL PITUITARY

Creation

Action

Stand behind the person to work on the head. You do not need to be on the reflexes of the head.

Work from approximately 2cm behind the hair line to the base of the skull. Work along the base of the skull and over the ears. When you reach the front of the ears, return to 2cm behind the hairline and repeat the procedure as often as you want to.

How to give a session of 'Metamorphosis' on the spine

When working on the spine, please use gentle pressure. You can also work at the side of the reflex point or place your hands over the reflexes.

Begin to work at the top of the spine (the 1st cervical vertebra) and continue down the spine to the coccyx.

The last corresponding point on the spine is at the base of the spinal column, the coccyx. You or the recipient may not be comfortable touching this area. If so, place your hands over this point. Follow the link to view a demonstration on youtube. https://www.youtube.com/watch?v=NW3e2kNi8CU

'Metamorphosis' and Pregnancy

It is not recommended to hold the reflexes on the ankles if the recipient is pregnant; using the circular movement will avoid stimulating the ankle reflexes. 'Metamorphosis' can benefit the mother and baby. However, there is some debate that stimulating the ankle reflexes using the thumb to apply pressure may promote labour as those reflexes are associated with the uterus and ovaries.

As a Reflexologist St. John would have been knowledgeable of this. He did not advise caution as he did not consider his work to be massage. 'Metamorphosis' has a different intention and touch. We are not massaging or pressing with any firmness.

Working with babies and young children

Children and babies are given 'Metamorphosis' by someone acting as a catalyst, yet it is still the child's inner principle of life that affects the change.

A baby can have a short session from birth. They only need a few minutes on the feet, hands and head as the traits are not embedded yet.

The Anterior fontanel, known as the soft spot, is on top of the baby's head toward the front. Four bones on the area do not join because they have rounded corners. The soft spot may close as early as nine months of age or as late as two years. Use a light touch when working with babies. Alternatively, place your hands over the head if you wish.

The length of time spent working with young children depends entirely on how long and how often they will allow you. When children have had enough they will let you know by pulling away. Usually, ten to fifteen minutes should be sufficient.

Working with the Elderly

Some people do not treat the elderly or terminally ill because they fear sessions will make them go forward to pass on. They may be mentally preparing for this anyway. If this happens, remember you did not influence this decision, their innate intelligence did. A person would not allow changes that were not beneficial to them; the sessions may help them depart peacefully.

Mixing Therapies

Mixing therapies is a controversial subject. Many people believe you should not mix therapies and others are happy to do so. It is up to each person to interpret this as they wish. Donna Armanasco covers the subject in detail.

Donna Armanasco (2015) explained,

> Robert believed that if a person approaches you for 'Metamorphosis' and that person is already receiving some form of therapy; it is acceptable for them to have 'Metamorphosis' as their innate intelligence accepts the therapy as part of the person.

> In 'Metamorphosis', the person is re-orientating with the self from their inner motivation and ability to heal. In nearly all other practises, the motivation to heal stems from sources outside the self, Universal energy, the will of the practitioners, remedies, medicines, which all do for the client the opposite to 'Metamorphosis'.

> Also, Donna Armanasco explained that starting another therapy after they have started sessions of 'Metamorphosis' can potentially be a problem.

We never tell a person not to have other treatments. Many treatments and therapies work on the physical body promoting relaxation, relieving stress and boosting energy levels. They will not interfere with 'Metamorphosis'.

Some therapies require the person to be attuned before they can heal clients and themselves. If a person is involved in a therapy that requires them to have attunement, they should have the attunements before they start 'Metamorphosis'. As Donna Armanasco explained the person's innate intelligence would then accept they are part of the person.

I feel if a person is using a therapy that teaches self-healing methods, for example Reiki healing, and they are giving themselves healing with that method they should initially consider using 'Metamorphosis' while having the sessions. They can resume the other therapies at a later date. Whether to use different methods simultaneously would be the individual's choice.

Case Studies

We cannot keep case studies with 'Metamorphosis' because we do not know what happens within the person.

The person is healing themselves. Your only motive is to help them.

Some people feel the need to see changes that have taken place in another person as evidence they are doing things correctly. They are looking for a visible difference, something tangible, but this may not be apparent.

We are not treating symptoms or looking for a cure, and we cannot take responsibility or credit for changes that occur.

You cannot look for visible changes in people or expect them to tell you something has changed. The person's innate intelligence is doing the work, any motivation or intent you may have will not affect the outcome.

Asking the person how they feel or what changes have taken place will lead them to expect changes to occur, leading to self-doubt.

If you need people to regard you as someone responsible for a person's transformation, you will realise it is different when you understand the true essence of 'Metamorphosis'. It is not about our motives or needs. When you see a person changing and living their life to their full potential, you will know it was due to their inner being that change has taken place. Outside influences played no part in the result.

However, during a session you may experience events that confirm St. John's theory, I feel it is good to share those experiences as they are not case studies but observations.

An example of this is an elderly client who told me he had not spoken to his father for most of his adult life. While I was working on the area around the first joint of the big toe which represents the father principle, the client began to speak of his father.

In his time it was common for people to take their shoes to a shoemaker for repair. The shoemaker used a mould in the shape of the human foot. Many families would buy a mould as it was more economical to do the repairs themselves. He recalled watching his father working on the shoes and spoke fondly of him. The client's wife was looking at him in amazement.

Afterwards, she asked "Do you realise you spoke about your father? That is the first time you have mentioned him in years." He replied, "I know that was very strange, but I just felt that I wanted to speak about him."

It is usual for people to talk about their parent's. I was not aware of this at my first session, but I also spoke about my father.

'Metamorphosis' and Autism

From a 'Metamorphosis' point of view autism is an extreme afference. The person compulsively retreats into themselves. The compulsion of their pattern means they have no choice but to be out of life. They are often in a constant state of hypersensitivity and fraught with frustration. They find it difficult, or are unable to make eye contact.

'Metamorphosis' can help orientate them by easing the tensions and perhaps give them some inner calm and peace.

'Metamorphosis' and Bipolar

People with Bipolar experience mood swings. They swing between afference and efference.

Afference is the phase when they are quiet, calm and withdrawn. They tend to be careful with their budget, think everything through carefully and take little action in most areas of their lives.

Efference is the phase when they act without thinking and behave irrationally. In this phase people make impulsive purchases or decisions without thinking about the consequences of their actions. Sessions of 'Metamorphosis' balance the afference and efference in a person.

'Metamorphosis' and Down syndrome

St. John had great success working with children with Down syndrome.

I asked Donna Armanasco to clarify the stories circulating that St. John had reversed Down syndrome by working on a baby from a young age.

Donna Armanasco (2015) explained,

> Robert did work with a baby with Down syndrome from birth. He told the story many times. However, I never heard the bit about her going on to be a great scholar embellishment. When Robert was teaching, there were quite a few mothers' there with their babies with Down syndrome. Robert asked me to go to one and work on the head of this baby for a bit. So, I did. The baby fell into a state of what seemed unconscious and increasingly became more and more Down syndrome in looks. After a while, it started to come out of that state, and as it did, it looked less and less Down syndrome. I have to say it was quite something to see. And that was just from working on the baby's head for a few minutes. In short, we do tend to work on babies for a much shorter time.

Donna Armanasco confirmed St. John would not have claimed to have reversed the condition as they did not see this infant again.

St. John taught that for 'Metamorphosis' to work on a person, we should not label them. You are not treating a person's condition. You are seeing a person as a whole.

If you label the person, you are treating a symptom instead of a person. If you are looking to cure a person, this implies you are looking to remove a symptom. 'Metamorphosis' removes the cause of the symptom.

Frequently Asked Questions

Do I need a particular setting?

All that is required are two chairs or a settee. Playing soothing music or burning candles while working will not make any difference to the outcome of a session. Still a person will enjoy the relaxed atmosphere and appreciate you have created a tranquil space.

Should I ground myself before a session?

Grounding will not make any difference to the outcome. As you become attuned you may not feel the need to protect yourself. You will understand the essence of St. John's work and accept the sensations you feel. St. John advised to use one of the symbols before or after a session.

How many sessions can a person have?

You cannot pre-empt how many sessions will be required.

'Metamorphosis' is unique. Only the person will know how many sessions they will need; you have to let them decide.

Sometimes, people will say they do not need another session and later they will get in touch and ask for a session as they have completed the previous changes and are ready to go forward again.

How long does a session last?

To tell a person how long they need to work is controlling and imposing rules. How can we know how long a person would require you to work on an area?

I have read teachings advising the feet should be worked on for approximately 20 minutes each and the hands for 5 minutes ending the session by working on the head for a few minutes.

Why are the feet more important than the hands? Why is the head so unimportant it only needs a few minutes spent on it?

The head allows a person to make sense of the new patterns of behaviour emerging because of 'Metamorphosis' and deal with the changes happening to their inner being. So, it is just as important as the feet and hands.

'Metamorphosis' is unlike other modalities. You cannot give it structure or time its duration. Many people are spontaneous and can follow their instincts during a session. Some people will expect the learning to be structured so they can follow instructions.

Everyone is free to see it from their perspective, making it difficult for a person who needs structure in their training to understand the principle of the work.

Now, let's look at the procedure and how it can work within a time frame.

If you are working on yourself, family or friends, you will work at your own pace, interacting with the person as you work.

It will differ for practitioners; they will need to work within a time frame. Most adults will not need an hour-long session; 40 to 55 minutes may be sufficient. A guideline is to begin with suggesting approximately an hour per session. You will spend some of that time getting into a comfortable position before commencing.

How long should you work on each area?

You work in a way that is best for you and the recipient.

You may feel the person is not responding to their present situation, so decide to do more work on the right foot. This represents what they are dealing with at present, before proceeding to the left foot, which deals with the past.

You may feel the person needs more time spent on their left foot to release the past blockages as soon as possible. The same applies to the hands.

You will learn as you practice when it is time to move on, but do not worry about not doing things right. There is no right or wrong way. Move on when you feel ready.

If you have covered all the areas and feel you need to spend more time, you can go back to an area and work on it again.

Just enjoy the session. The person's innate intelligence will know how to react for their benefit.

Do you relate to a person?

There are no hard and fast rules. Each person is an individual and will respond in their own way. You may find some people become so relaxed they fall asleep. Others sit quietly and enjoy the session. If the person wishes to speak to you, that is fine. Some ask questions and feel reassured when you answer them.

Can I give myself 'Metamorphosis'?

You can work on yourself as often as you feel you need to. Use your fingers to touch your reflex points the same as you would with another person.

Can a person with specific ailments benefit?

'Metamorphosis' does not claim to cure or help with specific ailments. It simply changes patterns inherited at conception. The inherited patterns cause the symptoms, so removing the patterns can mean the symptoms cease.

Can you send 'Metamorphosis' to another person?

The principle of correspondence that everything reflects every other thing is used to send distance healing.

Choose an object to represent the person, for example a doll, or a pillow. St. John used a plaster cast of a foot. Alternatively, you can visualise the person as you send healing.

'Metamorphosis' works with the person's innate intelligence, and only the recipient knows how many sessions they will need.

It appears to me it is essential that the person is aware you are sending 'Metamorphosis' to them so they can accept it. You will need them to tell you when to stop sending it.

As anyone can give themselves a 'Metamorphosis' session, it seems to defeat the purpose of sending it to them. If asked to send distance healing I prefer to teach them how to work on themselves.

However, this is the way I perceive it. If a person feels comfortable sending 'Metamorphosis' this way, that would be their choice.

Can you work on the Aura?

St. John referred to the Aura when he suggested you can place your hands above the head. This method is an option if you cannot touch the person, you place your hands over the head, hands and feet, but I always feel direct contact is a more natural approach.

Can two people work on the same person together?

For example, one person working on the right foot or hand, whilst the other person works on the left.

This practice would cause conflict for the person; they would be dealing with different patterns simultaneously.

Should a person remove their socks?

Working on a person with socks on will make no difference to the outcome of a session, but skin to skin contact allows you to observe the feet and is more direct.

Hand Symbols

Working on yourself with the more abstract hand symbols allows you to become your own healer.

Through the use of symbols, you communicate with the unconscious mind bypassing the intellect. You do not have to think about what the symbols are for. Your experiences while using them may differ each time.

You do not have to be in a calm place or state of mind to use the hand symbols. They address our fundamental patterns.

To use them in any way that creates structure alters the motive for using them and their relevance to 'Metamorphosis'. You can work with the symbols anytime and anywhere for as long and as often as you wish.

One day you may use one that completely relaxes you. Another day it may not feel right for you. Just experiment with them to find the one that you need at that time.

We all interpret the benefits differently. Use them to see what benefits you feel work with those you feel are right, not with ones you think you should use. Your inner being will tell you which one is right for you.

You can use the symbols in the air or in your lap, whichever feels more comfortable.

Crossed Fingers crossed at right angles (it does not matter which hand is on the top).

This symbol connects to the pineal gland situated at the top of the nail which receives the thought patterns in time and space.

Tipped Fingers. The tips of the fingers and thumbs touching.

This symbol connects to the pituitary gland situated at the base of the nail. The function is to interpret thought patterns to clarify them to the mind. The use of this symbol may calm and clarify your thoughts.

Conception Points. The middle finger of each hand touches the first joint of each thumb.

You are touching the area corresponding to the moment of conception.

A connection has now been created. Look into the space between the fingers and visualise the future.

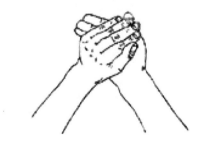

Cupped Hands. One hand cupped over the other (it does not matter which hand is on top).

The efferent pattern arrives at conception through our genes. These genes, having been subject to the thought patterns throughout generations bring thought patterns from the past into this new life.

The Spire. Fingers clasped together except the index fingers which are pointing upwards and the thumbs touching

The spire connects to the 'Thought Patterns of Time and Space'. This pattern starts at conception, the beginning of 'time' on this planet up to the present time.

We can undo or unhook from the trauma these patterns have on us.

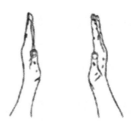

Creation Hand Symbol. Hands opposite each other, the distance between them is unimportant.

Afference and efference are the two elements essential to each other for true balance. This symbol creates the energy of oneness where afference and efference are not separate but equal.

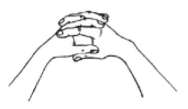

Creation Hand Symbol 11 Hands clasped together.

This hand symbol represents the state of oneness, a state of non-duality, where afference and efference are one. It brings our inner attention to the possibility of this and attunes us to it. The use of this symbol may help in times of loss and despair.

Below, Donna Armanasco clarifies the reason she added the Creation Hand Symbol 11.

Donna Armanasco (2017) explained,

> Just to explain about the 7th hand symbol. Robert had said that there was another hand symbol, but he couldn't see what it was. I cannot remember him saying that. After I got the news he died, I was very distressed and found myself in bed that night (or the next night, I can't remember) doing Meta to try and cope with the overwhelming distress I felt. I did my hands, feet, head, and the six hand symbols, and still the stress went on. Then I went into a sort of half-unconscious state, and without thinking, I found I had formed my hands in a particular position, and on doing so, the stress left me.

It was only when the stress lifted that I thought, what has happened and I realised I was holding my hands in a certain position. I immediately pulled my hands apart and thought, what am I doing? That is not a Meta hand symbol. The stress started to come back, so I put my hands back in the position, and the stress lifted again.

I was confused by what had happened (in fact, it was sometime later someone told me what Robert had said about a 7th hand symbol. Later other people told me the same thing, so I thought well, it might have been something he had said). At the time, I never told anyone what had happened because I felt I had no right to 'make' another hand symbol.

After some time and doing it regularly, I asked a friend of mine to try it and tell me what she experienced, and it was pretty much the same as me. I then asked another friend, and she said the same thing. I asked them not to tell anyone as I felt it was not my place to introduce another hand symbol into the practice of Meta.

Not sure how long it was before I started to get an understanding of what was happening when the hand symbol was done and the logic of it seemed to be in keeping with the Meta philosophy. Gradually I spoke to people about it. People who had been involved in Meta a long time and who knew Robert well. Eventually it became seen as a part of the Meta practice.

There was only one reason I eventually went forward with it, and that was because Robert had told me he felt I would take Meta to another level and encouraged me to take notes on my observations (at the time of him telling me this, I did not take much notice as it did not seem possible that I could make a contribution).

So, I put the two things together, that he had seen the coming of another hand symbol and that he had also told me I would somehow influence 'Metamorphosis'. In part because of the observations of others who had tried it - I took the big step of including it with Robert's hand symbols. It was a very difficult decision, but I bit the bullet and now have no regrets about taking such an action - although it did bother me for a long time.

How did St. John's work become confused with other methods?

Practitioners may be unaware that they are not always teaching St. John's work. Over time his work has been adapted and confused with other teaching methods.

This book may help to clarify St John's teachings so that we do not endorse other teaching as his.

Remaining detached is not St. John's teaching. St. John encouraged his students' to interact with the recipient. Relating to the person does not interfere with self-healing. You are not directing healing; their inner being receives the healing and uses it to change their inherited patterns. You cannot influence self-healing by remaining detached or relating to the person; it will not make any difference to the session outcome.

St. John did not teach squeezing the nail at the top and the base during a session.

You may have read that you should not touch your own feet, hands or head during a session as this will create a closed circuit; that you should use a cork or similar object to avoid contact between your hands and the reflexes you are touching. This is not St. John's teaching. He did not say that you should not touch your own feet, hands or head. If you cannot reach your feet or any other part, he suggested using something to reach that part, such as a ruler.

St. John did not teach the Universal Principles. He used two of the Universal Principles, namely the principle of Mentalism, everything is in the mind, the Universe is Mental, everything starts as an idea, and the principle of Correspondence that everything reflects everything. The reflex points and spine correspond with the gestation period which reflects life itself. However, the Universal Principles were not a part of his teachings.

St. John never used the analogy of the caterpillar emerging into a butterfly to describe 'Metamorphosis'. 'Metamorphosis' is the bringing of something into being which has never existed before. The butterfly is a prescribed process. It emerges into a butterfly still carrying the 'blockages' it had as a caterpillar. In that respect nothing has changed except its appearance.

'Metamorphosis' goes beyond transformation to the freedom to transmute. Some people say they do not like the word transmute as they are not sure of its meaning. It simply means to change the form or nature of a thing or person into a completely different one.

After 'Metamorphosis' a person does not become another version of who they were. They are free of the old inherited behaviour patterns and cannot revert to being the person they were before.

We now know a baby is aware of what is happening outside of the womb during the gestation period.

You may read that everything the mother experiences during the pregnancy is responsible for the baby's future behaviour patterns. St. John taught that blockages are with us from conception. We cannot inherit them after conception.

However, if the baby's environment is unsympathetic or frightening during the gestation period the blocks become more established.

Information about the International Metamorphosis Association

We offer a home study program and our tutors hold study days worldwide.

Some students learn 'Metamorphosis' to benefit themselves or family and friends. Others learn because they want to become practitioners or hold study days to teach others.

Students attending a study day or taking the home study course do not have to join the association. They are free to practice or teach 'Metamorphosis'.

Students are not required to purchase any additional reading material and there are no hidden extras.

There is no agenda. However, feedback and suggestions from members are always welcome.

We simply invite 'Metamorphosis' practitioners worldwide to join us in giving insight into Robert St. John's work whilst adhering to his teachings and principles.

Robert St. John disapproved of governing bodies, the definition being a group of people appointed to supervise and regulate a field of activity or institution. Governing bodies impose rules and conditions for members. Robert St. John said there are no rules in 'Metamorphosis'. He also disapproved of paying fees to organisations to practise and teach his work.

He believed that once a person had the knowledge and felt they truly understood the essence of 'Metamorphosis', they should be free to practice it on themselves and others as they interpret it.

The International Metamorphosis Association is not a governing body. We are an association; a group of people joined together for a purpose. Our purpose is to enhance people's knowledge of Robert St. John's work. He did not impose any rules; we follow his teaching.

'Metamorphosis' is safe. No harm can befall a person. However, we would recommend that you consider Professional Liability Insurance as a safeguard. We have sourced companies that cover 'Metamorphosis' if our members wish to avail themselves of it.

Should you be interested in our aims and code of practice we are happy to answer any questions.

For further information and contact details please refer to the following website

- https://www.theinternationalMetamorphosisassociation.com
- email: courses@cytanet.com.cy
- email: mail@therapytraining4u.com

Recommended Reading

Robert St. John wrote several books that are available via this link:

- www.metamorphosis-rsj.com

References

- Armanasco, D. (2015) Email to Patricia Newman, 22nd July
- Armanasco, D. (2015) Email to Patricia Newman, 30th July.
- Armanasco, D. (2015) Email to Patricia Newman, 31st July.
- Armanasco, D. (2015) Email to Patricia Newman, 16th August
- Armanasco, D. (2017) Email to Patricia Newman, 16th November.

The International Metamorphosis Association T/A Therapy

training4u.com®